ADEOLA

LEADERSHIP & MANAGEMENT

Understanding the principles involved

All rights reserved. No part of this publication may be reproduced, stored in a retrieval system, or transmitted in any form or by any means without the prior permission in writing of the author or as expressly permitted by law, or under terms agreed with the appropriate reprographics rights organisation. Enquiries concerning reproduction outside the scope of the above should be sent to the author of this book at the address below. You must not circulate this book in any other binding or cover and you must impose this same condition on any acquirer.

Printed in the United States of America

© Adeola Babatunde 2013

www.adeolababatunde.com

info@adeolababatunde.com

ISBN 978-1-4716-0748-6

Published By:

David Daniels Consultancy Ltd

CONTENTS

What is Leadership? 4

What is Management? 13

Is there any difference between Leaders and Managers? 29

Qualities of a good Leader 44

Dealing with challenges as a Leader 58

Notes 63

CHAPTER 1

WHAT IS LEADERSHIP?

Leadership and management are not the same. To be a leader, one needs an exclusive set of human relations and interpersonal skills. Its essence is being able to influence. To influence, one needs a number of component skills. Some are fairly easy to develop - others take a long time to protect. To get from A to B one can choose many different ways. for example one can ride a bicycle or fly a plane. One is easy to learn but not so fast. The other is fast but not easy to learn. For example, you can use your authority, it's quick. But learning charisma takes more time but is more powerful.

It is not an easy task to define leadership and come up with a "one size fits all" leadership definition, despite the vast amount of research and information on the subject.

There are many great leaders in the world today and yet they can be very different in their style and ways of working. This makes it hard to know where to start, if you want to develop your leadership skill!

Who is a Leader? We do know that leaders inspire others and are good communicators. They quickly appraise situations and the relationships involved. They know when to act quickly and when it is better to involve others in decision making. For example, if a business is losing money, then someone with a more authoritative leadership style is necessary. This requires an individual who is not afraid to make fast, sometimes painful decisions and whose ability to steer a path forward is respected by others.

If a business is stagnant, then someone with a facilitative leadership style which involves others, encourages creativity and fosters change is essential.

A leadership definition is further complicated by the fact that a good leader is like a chameleon; he or she will change their approach depending on the situation.

Good leaders tend to be very perceptive and aware of the needs of the business and its employees. They find out when to direct and when to delegate to employees. When involved in a project, they place more emphasis on the relationship of those involved to achieve results, than on projections and timelines.

How do we create a proper definition of a leader? What are their qualities? Remember that good leaders are not always found in high places. I once worked for a company where important decisions were discussed with someone in a low level of management. A good leader must have the ability to inspire others and instinctively know how to approach people in getting the best response. Having a greater awareness of the traits of good leaders will allow you to develop your own definition of what leadership is. Build these traits into your own style of working to make a real difference to your leadership in the workplace.

What is Leadership?

8 main leadership styles :

1. **Autocratic:** The leader takes the decisions and announces them, expecting subordinates to carry them out without question.

2. **Persuasive:** At this point on the scale, the leader also takes all the decisions for the group without discussion or consultation but believes that people will be better motivated if they are persuaded that the decisions are good ones. He or she does a lot of explaining and 'selling' in order to overcome any possible resistance to what he or she wants to do. The leader also puts a lot of energy into creating enthusiasm for the goals he or she has set for the group.

3. **Consultative:** In this style the leader confers with the group members before taking decisions and, in fact, considers their advice and their feelings when framing decisions. He or she may, of course, not always accept the subordinates' advice but they are likely to feel that they can have some influence. Under this leadership style the decision and the full responsibility for it remain with the leader .

4. **Democratic:** Using this style, the leader would characteristically lay the problem before his or her subordinates and invite discussion. The leader's role is that of conference leader, or chairman, rather than that of decision taker. He or she will allow the decision to emerge out of the process of group discussion, instead of imposing it on the group as the boss. What distinguishes this approach from

previous discussions of leadership style is that there will be some situations in which each of the above styles is likely to be more appropriate than the others.

5. **Telling:** In an emergency, a telling style may be most appropriate and would normally be considered justified by the group (as long as the general climate of that group is supportive and mature).

6. **Selling:** The selling style would tend to fit situations in which the group leader possesses all the information on which the decision must be based and calls for a very high level of commitment and enthusiasm on the part of group members if the task is to be carried through successfully.

7. **Consulting:** The consulting style is likely to be most appropriate when there is time to reach a considered decision and when the information on which the decision needs to be based lies among the members of the group.

8. **Joining:** The joining style is appropriate under similar conditions, with an exception that this is likely to be appropriate where the nature of the responsibility associated with the decision is such that group members are willing to share it with their leader, or alternatively the leader is willing to accept responsibility for decisions which he or she has not made personally.

What is Leadership?

Leadership is a fascinating subject for many people. The term conjures up a familiar scene of a powerful, heroic, triumphant individual with a group of followers returning home after winning a national championship or a war against the evil enemy. They all march through town surrounded by a crowd waving flags. Or an enthusiastic orator, who delivers an energetic speech with hands waving in the air, to thousands of people gathered in a plaza.

The widespread fascination with leadership may be because of the impact that leadership has on everyone's life. Stories of heroic leadership go back thousands of years: Moses delivering thousands of Hebrews from Egypt or Alexander the Great building a great empire. Why were certain leaders able to inspire and mobilise so many people, and how did they achieve what they achieved? There are so many questions to which we want answers, but many remain as puzzling as ever. In recent decades, many researchers have undertaken a systematic and scientific study of leadership.

Leadership is defined in so many different ways that it is hard to come up with a single working definition. Leadership is not just a person or group of people in a high position; understanding leadership is not complete without understanding interactions between a leader and his or her followers. Neither is leadership merely the ability or static capacity of a leader. We need to look into the dynamic nature of the relationship between leader and followers. In these unique social dynamics, all the parties involved attempt to influence each other in the pursuit of goals.

These goals may or may not coincide: Participants actively engage in defining and redefining the goal for the group and for themselves.

In a comprehensive statement: Leadership is a process in which a leader attempts to influence his or her followers to establish and accomplish a goal or goals. In order to accomplish the goal, the leader exercises his or her power to influence people. That power is exercised in earlier stages by motivating followers to get the job done and in later stages by rewarding or punishing those who do or do not perform to the level of expectation.

Leadership is a continuous process, with the accomplishment of one goal becoming the beginning of a new goal. The proper reward by the leader is of utmost importance in order to continually motivate followers in the process.

What does leadership do for an organisation? If we define leadership as a process involving interactions between a leader and followers, usually subordinate employees of a company, leadership profoundly affects the company: It defines or approves the mission or goal of the organisation. This goal setting is a dynamic process for which the leader is ultimately responsible. A strong visionary leader presents and convinces followers that a new course of action is needed for the survival and prosperity of the group in the future. Once a goal is set, the leader assumes the role of ensuring successful accomplishment of the goal. Another vital role of leadership is to represent the group/organisation and link it to the external world in order to obtain vital resources needed to carry out its mission and when necessary, leadership has to defend the organisation's integrity.

Leadership in a Multicultural Community

One major situational factor is the cultural values of the followers. People who have different cultural norms and values require different leadership styles. In a highly collective society such as Japan, the Philippines, Guatemala, or Ecuador, where the social bond among members is very strong and people look out for one another, a strong patriarch at the top of the social hierarchy tends to emerge as an effective leader. Such a leader is not only accepted by the followers but is also expected to protect their interests. China's Deng Xiao-Ping, whose influence continues even after his death, is a case in point.

On the other hand, in an extremely individualistic society, such as the United States where the social bonds are loose and individuals are expected to take care of themselves, success and achievement are admired, and a competitive and heroic figure is likely to emerge as a leader. It is no surprise that John F. Kennedy became such a charismatic figure in the United States. His energetic and inspirational speeches are still vividly remembered. Regardless of culture and time, however, a great leader is remembered for his or her charisma, which means "divinely inspired gift" in Greek.

Charismatic leaders have profound effects on followers. Through their exceptional inspirational and verbal ability, they articulate ideological goals and missions, communicate to followers with passion and inspiration, set an example in their own behaviours, and demand hard work and commitment from followers, above and beyond normal expectation.

Building on charismatic leadership, Bernard Bass (1985) proposed a theory of transformational leadership. Bass views leadership as a process of social exchange between a leader and his or her followers. In exchange for desired behaviours and task accomplishment, a leader provides rewards to followers. This nominal social exchange process is called transactional leadership. In contrast, a transformational leader places a higher level of trust in his or her followers and demands a much higher level of loyalty and performance beyond normal expectations. With unusual charismatic qualities and inspirational person-to-person interactions, a transformational leader transforms and motivates followers to make extra efforts to turn around ailing organisational situations into success stories. Lee Iacocca, when he took over Chrysler as CEO in 1979 and turned around this financially distressed company, was considered an exemplary transformational leader. He was able to convince many people, including employees and the U.S. Congress, to support the ailing company and to make it a success.

John Kotter (1988) distinguishes leadership from management. Effective management carefully plans the goal of an organisation, recruits the necessary staff, organises them, and closely supervises them to make sure that the initial plan is executed properly. Successful leadership goes beyond management of plans and tasks. It envisions the future and sets a new direction for the organisation. Successful leaders mobilise all possible means and human resources; they inspire all members of the organisation to support the new mission and execute it with enthusiasm. When an organisation faces an uncertain environment, it demands strong leadership. On the other hand, when an organisation faces internal operational complexity, it demands strong management. If an organisation faces both an uncertain environment and internal operational complexity, it requires both strong leadership and strong management.

CHAPTER 2

WHAT IS MANAGEMENT?

Traditional Interpretation of Management

There are a variety of views about this term. Traditionally, the term "management" refers to the set of activities, and often the group of people, involved in four general functions, including planning, organising, leading and coordinating activities. (Note that the four functions recur throughout the organisation and are highly integrated.)

Another Interpretation

Some writers, teachers and practitioners assert that the above view is rather outmoded and that management needs to focus more on leadership skills, e.g., establishing vision and goals, communicating the vision and goals, and guiding others to accomplish them. They also assert that leadership must be more facilitative, participative and empowering in how visions and goals are established and carried out. Some people assert that this really isn't a change in the management functions; rather it's re-emphasizing certain aspects of management.

What are the roles of a Manager?

Both of the above interpretations acknowledge the major functions of planning, organising, leading and coordinating activities -- they put different emphasis and suggest different natures of activities in the following four major functions.

They still agree that what managers do is the following:

1. Planning

Including identifying goals, objectives, methods, and resources needed to carry out methods, responsibilities and dates for completion of tasks. Examples of planning are strategic planning, business planning, project planning, staffing planning, advertising and promotions planning, etc.

2. Organising resources

To achieve the goals in an optimum fashion. Examples are organising new departments, human resources, office and file systems, re-organising businesses, etc.

3. Leading

Setting direction for the organisation, groups /individuals and also influence people to follow that direction. Examples are establishing strategic direction (vision, values, mission and / or goals) and championing methods of organisational performance management to pursue that direction.

4. Performance management processes

This occurs with the organisation's systems, processes and structures to effectively and efficiently reach goals and objectives. This includes on-going collection of feedback, monitoring and adjustment of systems, processes and structures accordingly. Examples include use of financial controls, policies and procedures, performance management processes, measures to avoid risks etc.

Another common view is that "management" is getting things done through others. Yet another view, quite apart from the traditional view, asserts that the job of management is to support employee's efforts to be fully productive members of the organisations' and citizens of the community. To most employees, the term "management" probably means the group of people (executives and other managers) who are primarily responsible for making decisions in the organisation. In a non-profit, the term "management" might refer to all or any of the activities of the board, executive director and/or programme directors.

Problem Solving Skills

Much of what managers and supervisors do is solve problems and make decisions. New managers and supervisors, in particular, often solve problems and decisions by reacting to them. They are "under the gun", stressed and very short for time. Consequently, when they encounter a new problem or decision they must make, they react with a decision that seemed to work before. It's easy with this approach to get stuck in a circle of solving the same problem over and over again. Therefore, as a new manager or supervisor, get used to an organised approach to problem solving and decision making. Not all problems can be solved and decisions made by the following, rather rational approach. However, the following basic guidelines will get you started. Don't be intimidated by the length of the list of guidelines. After you've practiced them a few times, they'll become second nature to you -- enough that you can deepen and enrich them to suit your own needs and nature. (Note that it might be more your nature to view a "problem" as an "opportunity". Therefore, you might substitute "opportunity" for "problem" in the following guidelines.)

1. Define the problem

This is often where people struggle. They react to what they think the problem is. Instead, seek to understand more about why you think there's a problem.

Identifying the problem:

"The following should be happening, but isn't ..." or "The following is happening and should not ..." As much as possible, be specific in your description, including what is happening, where, how, with whom and why. (It may be helpful at this point to use a variety of research methods.

Identifying complex problems:

If the problem still seems overwhelming, break it down by repeating steps a-f until you have descriptions of several related problems.

Verifying your understanding of the problems:

It helps a great deal to verify your problem analysis by conferring with a peer or someone else.

Priorities the problems discovered:

If you discover that you are looking at several related problems, then priorities which ones you should address first.

Note the difference between "important" and "urgent" problems. Often, what we consider to be important problems to consider are really just urgent problems. Important problems deserve more attention. For example, if you're continually answering "urgent" phone calls, then you've probably got a more "important" problem and that's to design a system that screens and prioritises your phone calls.

Understand your role in the problem:
Your role in the problem can greatly influence how you perceive the role of others. For example, if you're very stressed out, it'll probably look like others are, too, or you may resort too quickly to blaming and reprimanding others. Or, you feel very guilty about your role in the problem and you ignore the accountabilities of others.

2. Look at potential causes of the problem
a. It's amazing how much you don't know about what you don't know. Therefore, in this phase, it's critical to get input from other people who notice the problem and who are affected by it.
b. Write down what your opinions are and what you've heard from others.
c. Regarding what you think might be performance problems associated with an employee; it's often useful to seek advice from a peer or your supervisor in order to verify your impression of the problem.
d. Write down a description of the cause of the problem and in terms of what is happening, where, when, how, with whom and why.

3. Identify alternatives for approaches to resolve the problem
At this point, it's useful to keep others involved (unless you're facing a personal and/or employee performance problem). Brainstorm for

solutions to the problem. Very simply put, brainstorming is collecting as many ideas as possible, then screening them to find the best idea.

It's critical when collecting the ideas not to pass any judgment on the ideas -- just write them down as you hear them. (A wonderful set of skills used to identify the underlying cause of issues is systems thinking.)

4. Select an approach to resolve the problem

a. Which approach is the most likely to solve the problem for the long term?

b. Which approach is the most realistic to accomplish for now?

c. Do you have the resources?

d Are they affordable?

e. What is the extent of risk associated with each alternative? (The nature of this step, in particular, in the problem solving process is why problem solving and decision making are highly integrated?)

5. Plan the implementation of the best alternative

a. Carefully consider "What will the situation look like when the problem is solved?"

b. What steps should be taken to implement the best alternative to solving the problem?

c. What systems or processes should be changed in your organisation,? For example, a new policy or procedure don't resort to solutions where
   someone is "just going to try harder".

d How will you know if the steps are being followed or not? (these are your indicators of the success of your plan)

1

e. What resources will you need in terms of people, money and facilities?

f. How much time will you need to implement the solution? Write a schedule that includes the start and stop times.

(An important aspect of this step in the problem-solving process is continual observation and feedback.)

6. Monitor the indicators of success:

a. Are you seeing what you would expect from the indicators?

b. Will the plan be done according to schedule?

c. If the plan is not being followed as expected, then consider:

    1. Was the plan realistic?

    2. Are there sufficient resources to accomplish the plan on schedule?

    3. Should more priority be placed on various aspects of the plan?

    4. Should the plan be changed?

7. Verify if the problem has been resolved or not

One of the best ways to verify if a problem has been solved or not is to resume normal operations in the organisation. Still, you should consider;

a. What changes should be made to avoid this type of problem in the future? Consider changes to policies and procedures, training, etc.

b. Lastly, consider "What did you learn from this problem solving?"

c. Consider writing a brief memo that highlights the success of the problem solving effort, and what you learnt as a result. Share it with your supervisor, peers and subordinates.

Management and planning

Planning typically includes use of the following basic terms. NOTE: It's not critical to grasp completely accurate definitions of each of the following terms. It's more important for planners to have a basic sense for the difference between goals/objectives (results) and strategies/tasks (methods to achieve the results).

1. Goals

Goals are specific accomplishments that must be accomplished in total, or in some combination, in order to achieve some larger, overall result preferred from the system, for example, the mission of an organisation. (Going back to our reference to systems, goals are outputs from the system.)

2. Strategies

These are the methods or processes required in total, or in some combination, to achieve the goals. (Going back to our reference to systems, strategies are processes in the system.)

3. Objectives

Objectives are specific accomplishments that must be accomplished in total, or in some combination, to achieve the goals in the plan.

Objectives are usually "milestones" along the way when implementing the strategies.

4. Implementation plan

Particularly in small organisations', people are assigned various tasks required to implement the plan.

5. Resources (and Budgets)

Resources include the people, materials, technologies, money, etc., required to implement the strategies or processes. The costs of these resources are often depicted in the form of a budget. (Going back to our reference to systems, resources are input to the system.)

The basic planning process

Whether the system is an organisation, department, business, project, etc., the basic planning process typically includes similar nature of activities carried out in similar sequence. The phases are carried out carefully or -- in some cases -- intuitively, for example, when planning a very small, straightforward effort. The complexities of the various phases (and their duplication throughout the system) depend on the scope of the system. For example, in a large corporation, the following phases would be carried out in the corporate offices, in each division, in each department, in each group, etc.

NOTE: Different groups of planners might have different names for the following activities and group them differently. However, the nature of the activities and their general sequence remains the same.

NOTE: The following are typical phases in planning. They do *not* comprise the complete, ideal planning process.

1. Mission

During planning, planners have in mind (consciously or unconsciously) some overall purpose or result that the plan is to achieve. For example, during strategic planning, it's critical to reference the mission, or overall purpose, of the organisation.

2. Stock taking

This "Stock taking" is always done to some extent, whether consciously or unconsciously. For example, during strategic planning, it's important to conduct an environmental scan. This scan usually involves considering various driving forces, or major influences, that might affect the organisation.

3. SWOT Analysis

For example, during strategic planning, planners often conduct a "SWOT analysis". (SWOT is an acronym for considering the organisations' **strengths** and **weaknesses**, and the **opportunities** and **threats** faced by the organisation.) During this analysis, planners also can use a variety of assessments, or methods to "measure" the health of systems.

4. Warding off threats

Based on the analysis and alignment for the overall mission of the system, planners establish a set of goals that build on strengths to take advantage of opportunities, while building up weaknesses and warding off threats.

5. Establish Strategies

The particular strategies (or methods to reach the goals) chosen depends on matters of affordability, practicality and efficiency.

6. Establish Objectives

Objectives are selected to be timely and indicative of progress towards goals.

7. Associate Responsibilities and time lines with each Objective

Responsibilities are assigned, including for implementation of the plan, and for achieving various goals and objectives. Ideally, deadlines are set for meeting each responsibility.

8. Write and Communicate a Plan Document

The above information is organised and written in a document which is distributed around the system.

9. Celebrate Accomplishment of the Plan

This step is frequently forgotten, which can lead to increasing frustration and skepticism on the part of those people who are responsible to carry out the plan.

How to identify Successful Planning and Implementation

A common failure in many kinds of planning is that the plan is never really implemented. Instead, all focus is on writing a plan document.

Too often, the plan sits collecting dust on a shelf. Therefore, most of the following guidelines help to ensure that the planning process is carried out completely and is implemented completely -- or, deviations from the intended plan are recognised and managed accordingly.

1. Involve the Right People in the Planning Process

Going back to the reference to systems, it's critical that all parts of the system continue to exchange feedback in order to function effectively. This is true no matter what type of system. When planning, get input from everyone who will be responsible to carry out parts of the plan, along with representative from groups who will be affected by the plan. Of course, people also should be involved if they will be responsible to review and authorise the plan.

2. Write plans down and communicate them widely.

New managers, in particular, often forget that others don't know what these managers know. Even if managers do communicate their intentions and plans verbally, chances are great that others won't completely hear or understand what the manager wants done. Also, as plans change, it's extremely difficult to remember who is supposed to be doing what and according to which version of the plan. Key stakeholders (employees, management, board members, funders, investor, customers, clients, etc.) may request copies of various types of plans. Therefore, it's critical to write plans down and communicate them widely.

3. Goals and Objectives Should be SMARTER

SMARTER is an acronym, that is, a word composed by joining letters from different words in a phrase or set of words. In this case, a smarter goal or objective is:

Specific:

For example, it's difficult to know what someone should be doing if they are to pursue the goal to "work harder". It's easier to recognise "Write a paper".

Measurable:

It's difficult to know what the scope of "Writing a paper" really is. It's easier to appreciate that effort if the goal is "Write a 30-page paper".

Acceptable:

If I'm to take responsibility for pursuit of a goal, the goal should be acceptable to me. For example, I'm not likely to follow the directions of someone telling me to write a 30-page paper when I also have five other papers to write. However, if you involve me in setting the goal so I can change my other commitments or modify the goal.

Realistic:

Even if I do accept responsibility to pursue a goal that is specific and measurable, the goal won't be useful to me or others if, for example, the goal is to "Write a 30-page paper in the next 10 seconds".

Time-frame:

It may mean more to others if I commit to a realistic goal to "Write a

30-page paper in one week". However, it'll mean more to others (particularly if they are planning to help or guide me to reach the goal) if I specify that I will write one page a day for 30 days, rather than including the possibility that I will write all 30 pages on the last day of the 30-day period.

Extending:

The goal should stretch the performer's capabilities. For example, I might be more interested in writing a 30-page paper if the topic of the paper or the way that I write it will extend my capabilities.

Rewarding:

I'm more inclined to write the paper if the paper will contribute to an effort in such a way that I might be rewarded for my effort.

4. Building Accountability (Regularly Review Who's Doing What)

Plans should specify who is responsible for achieving each result, including goals and objectives. Dates should be set for completion of each result, as well. Responsible parties should regularly review status of the plan. Be sure to have someone of authority "sign off" on the plan, including putting their signature on the plan to indicate they agree with and support its contents. Include responsibilities in policies, procedures, job descriptions, performance review processes, etc.

5. Note Deviations from the Plan and Re-plan Accordingly

It's OK to deviate from the plan. The plan is not a set of rules. It's an overall guideline. As important as following the plan is, notice deviations and adjusting the plan accordingly.

6. Evaluate Planning Process and the Plan

During the planning process, regularly collect feedback from participants. Do they agree with the planning process? If not, what don't they like and how could it be done better? In large, on-going planning processes (such as strategic planning, business planning, project planning, etc.), it's critical to collect this kind of feedback regularly. During regular reviews of implementation of the plan, assess if goals are being achieved or not. If not, were goals realistic?

Do responsible parties have the resources necessary to achieve the goals and objectives? Should goals be changed? Should more priority be placed on achieving the goals? What needs to be done?

Finally, take 10 minutes to write down how the planning process could have been done better. File it away and read it the next time you conduct the planning process.

7. Recurring Planning Process is at Least as Important as the Plan Document

Far too often, primary emphasis is placed on the plan document. This is extremely unfortunate because the real treasure of planning is the planning process itself. During planning, planners learn a great deal from on-going analysis, reflection, discussion, debates and dialogue around issues and goals in the system. Perhaps there is no better example of misplaced priorities in planning than in business ethics. Far too often, people put emphasis on written codes of ethics and codes of conduct. While these documents certainly are important, at least as important is conducting on-going communications around these documents. The on-going communications are what sensitize people to understanding and following the values and behaviours suggested in the codes.

8. Nature of the process should be Compatible to nature of Planners

A prominent example of this type of potential problem is when planners don't prefer the "top down" or "bottom up", "linear" type of planning (for example, going from general to specific along the process of an environmental scan, SWOT analysis.

Mission, vision, values issues, goals, strategies, objectives, timelines, etc.) There are other ways to conduct planning.

9. Acknowledgement and Celebration of Results

It's easy for planners to become tired and even cynical about the planning process. One of the reasons for this problem is very likely that far too often, emphasis is placed on achieving the results. Once the desired results are achieved, new ones are quickly established. The process can seem like having to solve one problem after another, with no real end in sight. Yet when one really think about it, it's a major accomplishment to carefully analyse a situation, involve others in a plan to do something about it, work together to carry out the plan and actually see some results. So acknowledge this -- celebrate your accomplishment!

CHAPTER 3

IS THERE ANY DIFFERENCE BETWEEN LEADERS AND MANAGERS?

Comparison Chart

	Leadership	Management
Definition:	Leadership means "the ability of an individual to influence, motivate, and enable others to contribute toward effectiveness and success of the organisations' of which they are members."	Management comprises directing and controlling a group of one or more people or entities for the purpose of coordinating and harmonising that group towards accomplishing a goal.
Personality Styles:	Are often called brilliant and mercurial, with great charisma. Yet, they are also often seen as loners and private people. They are comfortable taking risks, sometimes seemingly wild and crazy risks. Almost all leaders have high levels of imagination	Tend to be rational, under control, problem solvers. They often focus on goals, structures, personnel, and availability of resources. Managers' personalities lean toward persistence, strong will, analysis, and intelligence.
Focus:	Leading people	Managing work

29

Outcomes:	Achievements	Results
Approach to tasks:	Simply look at problems and devise new, creative solutions. Using their charisma and commitment, they excite, motivate, and focus others to solve problems and excel.	Create strategies, policies, and methods to create teams and ideas that combine to operate smoothly. They empower people by soliciting their views, values, and principles. They believe that this combination reduces inherent risk and generates success
Approach to risk:	Risk-taking	Risk-averse
Role in decision-making:	Facilitative	Involved
Styles:	Transformational, Dictatorial, Authoritative, Consultative & Participative	Transactional, Autocratic, consultative, Democratic
Power through:	Charisma & Influence	Formal authority & Position
Organisation:	Leaders have followers	Manager have subordinate(s)
Appeal to:	Heart	Head

The debate between leadership and management has been raging for a number of years. "There is a profound difference between management and leadership, and both are important. To manage means to bring about, to accomplish, to take charge of, be responsible for, or to conduct. Leading is influencing, guiding in a direction, course, action or opinion. The distinction is crucial" - Warren Bennis

- The manager administers; the leader innovates.
- The manager is a copy; the leader is an original.
- The manager maintains; the leader develops.
- The manager focuses on systems and structure; the leader focuses on people.
- The manager relies on control; the leader inspires trust.
- The manager accepts reality; the leader investigates it.
- The manager has a short-range view; the leader has a long-range perspective.
- The manager asks how and when; the leader asks what and why.
- The manager has his or her eye always on the bottom line; the leader has his or her eye on the horizon.
- The manager imitates; the leader originates.
- The manager accepts the status quo; the leader challenges it.
- The manager is the classic good soldier; the leader is his or her own person.
- The manager does things right; the leader does the right thing.

This is a great list and it always causes me to pause to reflect on my own behaviour and ask "Where am I spending most of my time? Doing the left hand tasks or doing the right hand tasks?"

Another influential thinker on the distinction between management and leadership is John Kotter author of "John P. Kotter on What Leaders Really Do" in the book John makes the following observations:

- "Leadership and management are two distinctive and complementary systems of action. Both are necessary for success in an increasingly complex and volatile business environment."
- "Most U.S. corporations today are over managed and under led."
- "Strong leadership with weak management is no better, and is sometimes actually worse, than the reverse."
- "Management is about coping with complexity….. Without good management, complex enterprises tend to become chaotic… Good management brings a degree of order and consistency…."
- "Leadership, by contrast, is about coping with change…. More change always demands more leadership."
- "Companies manage complexity by planning and budgeting, by organising and staffing, and by controlling and problem solving.

By contrast, leading an organisation to constructive change involves setting a direction, aligning people, motivating and inspiring them to keep moving in the right direction."

I like the point that John Kotter makes when he says that "Leadership and management are two distinctive and complementary systems of action. Both are necessary for success in an increasingly complex and volatile business environment." The fact is that leadership and management are both important, they are two distinctive systems of action, both are necessary, and each seeks to do different things.

"The difference between managers and leaders, he wrote, lies in the conceptions they hold, deep in the psyches, of chaos and order. Managers embrace process, seek stability and control, and instinctively try to resolve problems quickly - sometimes before they fully understand a problem's significance. Leaders, in contrast, tolerate chaos and lack of structure and are willing to delay closure in order to understand the issues more fully in this way, Zalenznik argued, business leaders have much more in common with artists, scientists and other creative thinkers than they do with managers. Organisations need both managers and leaders to succeed, but developing both requires a reduced focus on logic and strategic exercises in favour of an environment where creativity and imagination are permitted to flourish."

In the end, we need to be good at leading first and managing second, the and why ..... then....... the how and the when!

Reflecting on your behaviour over the past month, ask yourself:

- Where do you find yourself spending the majority of your time? Managing or leading?

- Given that most organisations' are "over managed and under led", what two management tasks can you delegate this week? What two leadership behaviours do you need to focus on and improve this week?

WHAT IS THE HALLMARK OF A GOOD MANAGER?

The hallmark of a good Manager is effective delegation. Delegation is when a Manager gives responsibility and authority to subordinates to complete a task, and let the subordinates figure out how the task can be accomplished. Effective delegation develops people who are ultimately more fulfilled and productive. Managers become more fulfilled and productive themselves as they learn to count on their staffs and are freed up to attend to more strategic issues.

Delegation is often very difficult for new Managers, particularly if they have had to scramble to start the organisation or start a major new product or service themselves. Many managers want to remain comfortable, making the same decisions they have always made. They believe they can do a better job themselves. They don't want to risk losing any of their power and stature (ironically, they do lose these if they don't learn to delegate effectively). Often, they don't want to risk giving authority to subordinates in case they fail and impair the organisation.

However, there are basic approaches to delegation that, with practice, become the backbone of effective management and development. Thomas R. Horton, in *Delegation and Team Building: No Solo Acts Please* (Management Review, September 1992, pp. 58-61) suggests the following general steps to accomplish delegation:

1. Delegate the task to a particular person. This will increase motivation.

2. Assess the skills and capabilities of subordinates and assign the task to the most appropriate one.

3. Give information on what, why, when, who and where. You might leave the "how" to them. Write this information down.

4. Let the subordinate complete the task in the manner they choose, as long as the results are what the supervisor specifies. Let the employee have strong input as to the completion date of the project. Note that you may not even know how to complete the task yourself -- this is often the case with higher levels of management.

5. Ask the employee to summarise back to you, their impressions of the project and the results you prefer.

6. Get on-going non-intrusive feedback about progress on the project. This is a good reason to continue to get weekly, written status reports from all direct reports. Reports should cover what they did last week, plan to do next week and any potential issues.

7. Don't hover over the subordinate, but sense what they're doing and support their checking in with you along the way.

8. If you are not satisfied with the progress, continue to work with the employee and ensure they perceive the project as their responsibility.

9. Evaluate results more than methods.

10. Address insufficient performance and reward successes.

Internal Communications

Effective communication is the "life's blood" of an organisation. Organisations that are highly successful have strong communications. One of the first signs that an organisation is struggling is that communications have broken down. The following guidelines are very basic in nature, but comprise the basics for ensuring strong on-going, internal communications.

1 Have all employees provide weekly written status reports. Include what tasks were done last week, what tasks are planned next week, any pending issues and date the report. These reports may seem a tedious task, but they're precious in ensuring that the employee and their supervisor have mutual understanding of what is going on, and the reports come in very handy for planning purposes. They also make otherwise harried employees stand back and reflect on what they're doing.

2. Hold monthly meetings with all employees together. Review the overall condition of the organisation and review recent successes. Consider conducting "in service" training where employees take turns describing their roles to the rest of the staff. For clarity, focus and morale, be sure to use agendas and ensure follow-up minutes. Consider bringing in a customer to tell their story of how the organisation helped them. These meetings go a long way toward building a feeling of teamwork among staff.

3. Hold weekly or biweekly meetings with all employees. Have these meetings even if there is not a specific problem to solve -- just make them shorter. (Holding meetings only when there are problems to solve cultivate a crisis-oriented environment where managers believe their only job is to solve problems.) Use these meetings for each person to briefly give an overview of what they are doing that week. Facilitate the meetings to support exchange of ideas and questions. Again, for clarity, focus and morale, be sure to use agendas, take minutes and ensure follow-up minutes. Have each person bring their calendar to ensure scheduling of future meetings accommodates each person's calendar.

4. Have supervisors meet with their direct reports in one-on-one. This ultimately produces more efficient time management and supervision. Review overall status of work activities, hear how it's going with the supervisor and the employee, exchange feedback and questions about current products and services, and discuss career planning, etc. Consider these meetings as interim meetings between the more formal, yearly performance review meetings.

Designing Organisation and Staff

Overall, the organisation and its various groups should be organised in the configuration that reaches business goals in the most effective and efficient fashion. Guidelines in this section will help you ensure your organisation and its various groups are organised in the best configuration possible.

1. Conducting strategic planning to regularly review the purpose of your organisation, its overall goals and who should be doing what to meet those goals.

2. Using sound principles of employee performance management to regularly review what employees should be doing to produce results, how they're doing towards their results, and what must be done to help them do a better job of achieving results.

There are several problems that seem to keep coming up in small businesses, whether for-profit or non-profit.

NOTE: It is not always problems that provoke the need for organising. For example, if the organisation has been conducting strategic planning and produced new goals, these goals may require the organisation to reorganise. For example, if the business wants to expand market share in a certain region, then the organisation may need a new office in that region, more sales people, etc. Whether you're in an already established or a new organisation, the activity of organising and re-organising can be a major undertaking that has substantial effect on everyone in the organisation. Therefore, before we visit some specific guidelines for carrying out change, it's important to keep the following general principles in mind:

1. Take care of yourself first. Organisation-wide change can be highly stressful.

2. The process won't be an "aha!" It will likely not be as bad as you might expect, but won't be as good as you'd prefer either.

3. Keep perspective. Keep focused on meeting the needs of your customers.

4. Don't seek to control change, but rather to expect it, understand it.

5. Change is usually best carried out as a team-wide effort.

6. Communications about the change should be frequent and with all members.

7. To sustain change, the structures of the organisation itself should be modified, including strategic plans, policies and procedures.

Without visiting the overall purpose and goals, redesigning is usually a highly reactive and very short-term fix.

Therefore:

1. Carefully consider conducting a strategic planning process to guide you through reviewing your organisations' purpose.

2. Consider using a consultant. Ensure the consultant is highly experienced in organisation-wide change. Ask to see references.

3. Plan the change. How do you plan to reach the goals, what will you need to reach the goals, how long might it take and how will you know when you've reached your goals or not? What will you need in resources

and how much will they probably cost? Focus on the coordination of the departments/programmes in your organisation.

4. Document a plan. Forums should be held for organisation members to express their ideas for the plan. They should be able to express their concerns and frustrations as well. Note that plans do change. That's fine, but communicate that the plan has changed and why.

5. Include closure in the plan to acknowledge and celebrate your accomplishments.

6. Get as much feedback as practicable from employees during planning and implementation of the change, including what they think are the problems and what should be done to resolve them.

GUIDELINES FOR SELECTING A TEAM

1. Set clear goals for the results to be produced by the team. The goals should be designed to be "SMARTER", that is, be specific, measurable, acceptable to members, realistic, and have a time frame to be started and stopped, extend the capabilities of members and provide reward for their accomplishment. As much as possible.

2 Input from other members of the organisation when designing and wording these goals. Goals might be, for example, "produce a project report that specifies project plan, budget to develop and test a complete employee performance management system within the next year". Write

these goals down for eventual communication to and discussion with all team members.

3. Set clear goals for the effectiveness of the team process: The goals should also be designed to be "SMARTER". Goals might be, for example, attain 90% participation of all members during the first 6 weeks of weekly attendance, achieve 90% satisfaction ratings among members, each person takes at least one turn at facilitating the group, meetings start and stop on time, etc. Write these goals down for eventual communication to all team members.

4. Various types of teams have various purposes. Consider use of permanent teams, committees, self-directed teams, problem solving teams, etc.

5. Consider the extent of expertise needed to achieve the goals, including areas of knowledge and skills. Include at least one person who has skills in facilitation and meeting management. Attempt to include sufficient diversity of values and perspectives to ensure robust ideas and discussion. A critical consideration is availability -- members should have the time to attend every meeting.

6. Determine the structure of the Organisation. Structure includes the number of people in the group, how often they will meet and when and who will be the leader of the group.

7. Determine the process of the group. Depending on the nature of the results to be produced by the group, the process might be focused on

open discussion, action planning, problem solving and decision making, generating recommendations, etc.

8. Identify any need for training and materials. For example, members might benefit from brief overview of the stages of development of a team, receive training and packets of materials in regard to their goals and the structure and process of their team, etc.

9. Identify the costs to provide necessary resources for the team. Consider the cost of paying employees to attend the meeting, trainers and/or consultants, room rental, office supplies, etc.

10. In the first meeting, communicate the goals of the team, why each member was selected, the overall benefit of the goals to the organisation, the time frame for the team effort, who will lead the team (at least, initially), when the team might meet and where, etc.

11. Early on, plan team building activities to support trust and strong team. Team building activities can include, for example, a retreat in which members introduce themselves, exercises in which members help each other solve a short problem or meet a specific and achievable goal, extended period in which members can voice their concerns and frustrations about their team assignments, etc.

12. At this point, it's critical that supervisors remain available to provide support and resources as needed. Monitor that team goals are being met. Provide on-going encouragement and visibility to members. One of the most important forms of support a supervisor can provide is

coordination with other supervisors to ensure that team members are freed up enough to attend team meetings.

CHAPTER 4

QUALITIES OF A GOOD LEADER

The characteristics of a leader come through in our day to day interactions with those around us. Leaders come in all shapes, styles, and forms. If you stop to think about some of the leaders that have inspired you or even some that have infuriated you, the qualities of a good leader will become apparent.

When we think about the characteristics of a leader, we often think of leaders that are dynamic, which calls each of us to act or to follow. We could take an example, such as Hitler. He did not have the values that we should follow, but had that inspiration that could ignite a country. If we also stop to think about the leaders today in the USA, we do not get the same vision of a leader that has a dynamism that is hard to resist, but rather a leader that has that 'good to great' quality. Often times these leaders are more quiet and reserved, embodying the vision of good leadership skills and calling each of us to action in a subtle way that can often times leave us asking why we're buying what they're selling.

The answer is simple. The characteristics of a leader are not skills or behaviours that will be new to those that strive to master them, but will often times be the actions we all know we should be focused on, if we only had the time. Yes, developing good leadership skills takes time, just like perfecting an idea or delivering on a project. Without an investment of time, very few people will have the skills to become a great leader.

Let's examine some of these traits in more depth. The Santa Clara University and the Tom Peters Group noted the following characteristics as key characteristics of a leader. Don't be surprised if you don't find the complexity you were expecting as leadership is often promoted as that advanced skill few can attain.

Good Leadership qualities are:

- Honesty - Display sincerity, integrity, and candor in all your actions. Deceptive behaviour will not inspire trust.
- Competence - Your actions should be based on reason and moral principles. Do not make decisions based on childlike emotional desires or feelings.
- Forward-looking : Set goals and have a vision of the future. The vision must be owned throughout the organisation. Effective leaders envision what they want and how to get it. They habitually pick priorities stemming from their basic values.
- Inspiring - Display confidence in all that you do. By showing endurance in mental, physical, and spiritual stamina, you will inspire others to reach for new heights. Take charge when necessary.
- Intelligence - Read, study, and seek challenging assignments.
- Fair-mindedness - Show fair treatment to all people. Prejudice is the enemy of justice. Display empathy by being sensitive to the feelings, values, interests, and well-being of others.
- Broad-mindedness - Seek out diversity.

- Courageous - Have the perseverance to accomplish a goal, regardless of the seemingly insurmountable obstacles. Display a confident calmness when under stress.
- Straightforward - Use sound judgment to make good decisions at the right time.
- Imaginative - Make timely and appropriate changes in your thinking, plans, and methods. Show creativity by thinking of new and better goals, ideas, and solutions to problems. Be innovative!

As you can see, nothing revealed here is shocking, but skills we are all aware of, yet we take little time to practice. Again, developing good leadership skills does take practice and a great deal of time. If it were easy there would be far more leaders and far less managers.

A number of the characteristics of a leader fall into a greater category that many of the leading executives of today refer to as Emotional Intelligence. Achieving this level of leadership will inspire those around you and lead your team to great heights.

So what do you do with this 'new' information? It's time to refocus on your core as a leader and to spend your time wisely on what you value and the values of your organisation. It is easy to get caught up in the daily fires that pop up but this can be the downfall of aspiring leaders. To achieve a true leadership style you must be able to maintain these traits through good times and bad and to continually focus on the behaviours regardless of the situation.

An important aspect of good leadership is the ability to work and relate with others. When creating and building your unique leadership style, consistently developing relational skills is a priority. There are ten qualities that characterise successful leadership in the area of relating and communicating with other people.

1. Availability: A good leader is available and in touch with people. An important leadership skill is the ability to recognise needs and be able to respond to them quickly and in the moment.

2. Facilitating Harmonious Relationships: A good leader realises the importance of harmonious relationships and is proactive in creating a harmonious atmosphere. Successful results are born out of harmony rather than conflict. Good leadership wills priorities keeping conflict and disharmony to the minimum.

3. Approachability: A good leader is approachable and has an open door policy. Good leadership creates an environment where openness and honesty can occur in an atmosphere of fairness rather than judgment.

4. Appropriate use of authority: Sensitivity to the proper use, and conversely the misuse, of their authority is the hallmark of good leadership. A good leader will not use their position of authority for self-gratification and promotion or in a controlling and domineering manner. Successful leaders use their positional power with wisdom and sensitivity to the appropriateness of the circumstances.

5. Confidentiality: Good leaders conduct conferences and meetings in an atmosphere of trust. They display appropriate confidentiality and respect towards others and about others.

6. Self-Motivation and Development: Good leaders set and use goals to motivate themselves and others. They understand the importance of personal and professional development. Successful leaders do what is necessary to upgrade their knowledge and skills and be on the cutting edge in their field. Successful leaders not only motivate themselves in personal development but also motivate those around them.

7. Supportive: Good leaders are able to provide emotional support for those for whom they are responsible. They recognise the importance of encouragement and inspiring confidence and also give recognition of a job well done.

8. Maintaining Motivation and Team Spirit: A good leader provides incentives and motivators to improve the performance of their employees to challenge them to maintain quality results.

9. Clear Communication: A good leader is an excellent communicator. Their leadership involves communicating clearly the objectives and procedures required of a task. They set clear, attainable, and measurable goals.

10. An Understanding of Group Dynamics: A good leader understands the dynamics of group relationships. Successful leaders have the ability to lead groups without aggravating conflict and minimizing disharmony. They possess skills in creating a sense of team unity. They are adept at balancing the strengths and weaknesses of the group for best results. It is of prime importance to develop good relational skills as a leader.

A good leader is able to create in his team a desire to follow his leadership wholeheartedly.

Take these ten characteristics as a checklist to determine the strengths and weaknesses in your leadership style. Celebrate your strengths, focus on your weaker areas and start to work on them. In this way a good leader can develop into a great leader.

Behaviour and leadership

Character is central to good leadership - not just political leadership, but the leadership of Mums and Dads, Principals and Teachers, Managers and Administrators and everyone who influences lives around them.

According to General Norman Schwarzkopf;

"The main ingredient of good leadership is good character. This is because leadership involves conduct and conduct is determined by values." [Character]

Leadership is fundamentally about whom we are rather than what we are.

Followers who have trust in their leader's action show that trust by contributing to the organisation.

Burdensome compliance is counterproductive - it destroys trust and reduces commitment and willingness to accept responsibility.

The casualty is volunteerism - Willingness to contribute to the well-being of others or an organisation. Volunteerism is about "going the second mile."

As compliance increases volunteerism decreases. It is far better to build trust, respect followers and encourage the acceptance of responsibility.

Character provides the leader's deepest source of being and strongest source of restraint.

In many instances the first prompting to do "good" and the last barrier against doing wrong are the same - character. Character is both the motivation and the final restraint.

Character traits - integrity, respect and responsibility - are key components of good leadership.

These character traits - integrity, respect and responsibility - are observed in a leader's behaviour and manifested in a leader's relationships. Perhaps in recent decades there has been greater focus on the skills of management rather than the qualities of leadership. It is said that "managers are people who do things right while leaders are people who do the right thing."

Management requires skills and strategies but good leadership requires much more.

Good leadership requires good character.

No style of leadership is effective over time unless it is rooted in character that inspires trust and commitment. It is almost impossible to sustain anything, let alone leadership, over time unless it is of substance.

Fads and fashions all have their day. So too, do leadership styles. The best leaders have qualities that are rooted in character.

Good leaders:

- Are goal and people oriented
- Don't try and lead alone
- Listen to constructive criticism
- Accept responsibility
- Put the best interest of others before their own
- Are held accountable for the authority they exercise
- Lead by example
- Keep in touch with the work being undertaken
- Seek out wise advisers
- Are held accountable for the people they lead

Strength and goodness

Excellence, in a leadership context, is being the best person you can in terms of doing what is right for your organisation. This requires two qualities - strength and goodness - both are determined by character traits. These twin siblings of leadership - strength and goodness - parallel Lickona and Davidson's concept of "Smart and Good High Schools."

[Thomas Lickona and Matthew Davidson, State University of New York College, Cortland have developed the concept of "Smart and Good High Schools."

This concept of "smart and good'" high schools is extracted from the historical view that education has two goals - the mastery of skills and the building of character.

"Throughout history, and in cultures all over the world, education rightly conceived has had two great goals: to help students to become smart and to help them become good. They need character for both. They need character qualities such as diligence, a strong work ethic, and a positive attitude in order to do their best in school and succeed in life.

They need character qualities such as honesty, respect and fairness in order to live and work with others.'

There are parallels between the concept "good and smart" high schools and "good and strong" leadership. A leader's character is observed through their behaviour. A person of strong character shows drive, energy, determination, self-discipline, commitment, will-power and nerve.

A leader with these qualities attracts followers. On the other hand, a person of weak character does not display these qualities. They may be disorganised, vacillate or be inconsistent. A leader with these qualities does not attract followers.

A person of strong character can be either a good or a bad leader. A strong leader is not necessarily a good leader.

Think of Adolf Hitler, Robert Mugabe or Joseph Stalin in contrast to Mahatma Gandhi, Nelson Mandela or George Washington. Strong character is not necessarily coupled with good character.

*A gang leader is an example of a strong leader with a bad character while an outstanding community leader will have both strong and good character traits.

*Integrity, respect and responsibility are the three pillars of good leadership.

*Strong and good leadership and strong and good character are inextricably linked.

*Good leaders exercise authority wisely.

*Leadership inevitably involves the exercise of authority.

*Authority is the power to make people do as they are told. Authority, regardless of whether it is exercised by a policeman, a principal or Teacher, a team captain or a school monitor is never personally owned.

*It belongs to the position or office and is given on trust to be exercised with honesty, fairness and gentleness - integrity.

*The authority of a school principal is not personally owned but derived from the position and the school's board of trustees.

*The manner in authority if exercised influences the quality of leadership.

*The exercise of authority, like behaviour and leadership, is inextricably linked to character.

Strengthening a leader's character;

The eight cornerstone values - honesty, respect, responsibility, kindness, consideration, compassion, obedience and duty along with other character traits reproduce themselves as they are practiced. They are gained as they are given and given as they are gained.

Honesty, for examples spawns trust, respect and loyalty.

This explains why, when a school teaches cornerstone values definitions and backs that teaching up by advocating, modeling and having students experience them, the school culture is transformed.

In the same way a leader can transform his/her leadership by focusing on personal character traits.

The experience of everyone working with character education is that their own character is strengthened.

A simple worksheet is an effective way to action selected character traits.

Vision and articulation

One of the most important tasks any good leader must undertake is a personal assessment. An honest inventory of your skills, strengths and weaknesses can give insight into those areas that need improvement as well as those you should accept and learn to work around. A personal inventory also gives you the power of information which you can then use to create situations that emphasize your strengths for more consistently positive outcomes.

It is important to adopt a positive attitude throughout this task. You will want to record your strengths and weaknesses without judgment, but with an eye toward improvement. As the saying goes, "you cannot fix what you will not face." Remember too, that there is no cookie cutter leadership mound. Leaders are as different as the businesses they lead, and each brings different strengths to the task.

Compile your list in two columns taking care to make them somewhat even, include comments where appropriate. If you are having trouble coming up with strengths or weaknesses try the following:

• Ask a trusted friend or family member for some observations

• Review past employee evaluations you have received

• Administer on yourself the same evaluation you provide for employees

• Detail past successes and list the qualities you employed in those efforts

• Detail past failures and review what skills you could have used for a more successful outcome

• Put your list aside for a day or two

• If you are asked to offer consultations, lectures or papers, is there a topic or content pattern? (These may be strengths)

- Ask for feedback from employees

* List the personal qualities of leaders that you admire - which match your own? Which do you aspire to?

- Review leading journals/articles in your area - what gaps come to mind?

- Look for patterns in your work performance (for example, which tasks do you dread or avoid regularly)

- Write a detailed job description for a leader in your industry (or review the one you already have). Assess your comfort level or skill in each task area on a scale from one to five. You will not score perfect five in every area, nor should you expect to. The idea isn't to know it all, but to be a more effective leader by:

- Identifying, emphasizing and building on strengths

- Identifying, building up and/or working around weaknesses

- Creating a work environment that highlights your strengths

- Creating a team that complements your assets

- Developing a professional development learning plan

There may be some tasks or responsibilities that you are more comfortable delegating, that's perfectly okay. You will have more productive and satisfied employees if you are confident enough to let go and let them run with the tasks that emphasize their strengths.

Some weaknesses may require that you do some skill building. One example might be employee management. If you are shy, easily intimidated or don't communicate well, consider attending a workshop or working with a coach. Before you begin, priorities the areas you want to work on and identify specific goals for your development programme. It isn't enough to say that you want to improve your communication skills. How will that look?

What concrete steps will you take towards your goal each week? What is your timeline? Work on no more than two improvement areas at one time. Use a journal to track your progress and plan next steps. If it seems that your progress is slow or stagnant, you may need to rework your plan or learn to love yourself just as you are.

CHAPTER 5

DEALING WITH CHALLENGES AS A LEADER

"There is no way one person can be responsible for the success of an entire corporation," says Lepsinger. "Rational business-people know this, but there is something in the human psyche that makes us long for a saviour and our desire to pin all our hopes on one person--no matter how powerful, clever, or visionary--almost inevitably leads to disappointment. Sometimes it can even backfire in dramatic ways." Of course, few corporations are in the position to hire a high-profile leader themselves. But that doesn't mean it's a moot point for ordinary companies. The "cult of personality" spawned by the mythical celebrity leader has permeated all levels of business society. Both CEOs and those who follow them are influenced by this image.

PROBLEMS ASSOCIATED WITH BEING A LEADER ARE:

• **Over reliance on the leader to solve all the company's problems.** "Because no single leader has the necessary knowledge and expertise to solve difficult problems for an organisation, it is essential to involve other people with relevant knowledge and diverse perspectives," writes Lepsinger and Yukl. "However, members are unlikely to become involved if they believe the leader has superhuman abilities to single-handedly find the right path. Nor is high involvement likely to be encouraged by a leader with an exaggerated self-image who wants to appear to have all the answers."

*Exaggerated expectations lead to exaggerated disappointments.

When a celebrity leader is appointed the CEO for a troubled company, expectations and stock prices are dramatically raised, only to be rapidly deflated if no miracles occur shortly afterward. Consider what happened when Gary Wendt was selected to be the new CEO of the insurance company Conseco after a successful tenure running GE Capital. When the appointment was announced, Wendt was hailed as a saviour for Conseco, and its stock price rose by almost 50 per cent. The stock rose even more dramatically when he started issuing upbeat reports to investors.

However, just over two years later, Wendt stepped down, having failed to rescue Conseco from its doldrums. The stock sank by more than 99 per cent from its high, and Conseco was left with the burden of paying Wendt millions of dollars per year for the rest of his life."

· A single CEO misstep can have a catastrophic effect on profits. The previous example illustrates what can happen when a leader doesn't live up to expectations. But what happens to a company whose image is synonymous with that of its CEO when the said CEO commits a crime or some other high-profile *faux pas*? "Look no further than Martha Stewart," says Lepsinger. "Her company's stock prices fluctuated in tandem with the ups and downs of her insider-trading-conviction-sentencing-prison-release drama.

Like it or not, the stability of a company is inherently linked to the stability of the public image of the CEO. If your company has a celebrity leader, you'd better make sure he or she is a choirboy or choirgirl--and that no one even falsely accuses him or her of wrongdoing."

- **Celebrity CEOs are too sheltered to be fast on their feet.**

it is essential to understand what customers need, what competitors can do, and how potential customers view a company's products and services. Frontline personnel and lower-level managers will obtain much of this essential information long before it arrives in the senior executive's office. "

- **Frankly, employees don't want to be led by a figure on a white horse.** Too much emphasis on the wisdom and guidance of the sage-like leader doesn't sit well with today's workforce. Twenty-first century workers want to think for themselves, to formulate their own ideas, to feel in control of their own jobs. They don't want to follow orders. "Lee Iacocca, who embodied the old ideal of the charismatic, paternalistic CEO, was widely viewed as a great leader until his much more accessible and consultative successor, Bob Eaton, got dramatically better results at Chrysler," write the authors. "While Iacocca was effective in leading the company through the immediate crisis, his style of leadership was not the best one for rebuilding the company and preventing a similar crisis in the future."

So what's the bottom line? Lepsinger says that companies need to realise that effective leadership is not about glitz, glamour, and charisma; it's about results. "Real world" CEOs must have the flexibility to respond to continually changing conditions, the perspective to find an appropriate balance among competing demands, and the commitment to drive coordinated action by leaders ."CEOs must be concerned with organisational performance, with doing all the things it takes to close the gap between strategy and execution," he says.

"And here's the thing: these are skills that don't necessarily make sweet media stories and garner lots of camera time. They're behavioural. They are learnt, not inborn. There are no easy answers, just a lot of focused thinking and hard work--and realising that is the first step out of the star-struck land of the celebrity CEO and into the real world."

Some people still argue that we must replace management with leadership. This is obviously not so: they serve different, yet essential, functions. We need good management and we need more superb leadership. We need to be able to make our complex organisations' reliable and efficient. We need them to jump into the future - the right future - at an accelerated pace, no matter the size of the changes required to make that happens.

There are very, very few organisations' today that have sufficient leadership. Until we face this issue, understanding exactly what the problem is, we're never going to solve it. Unless we recognise that we're not talking about management when we speak of leadership, all we will try to do when we do need more leadership is work harder to manage.

At a certain point, we end up with over-managed and under-led organisations', which are increasingly vulnerable in a fast-moving world.

NOTES

NOTES

NOTES